W9-BGC-680

21st Century
Basic Skills
Library

WE CELEBRATE INDEPENDENCE DAY IN SUMMER

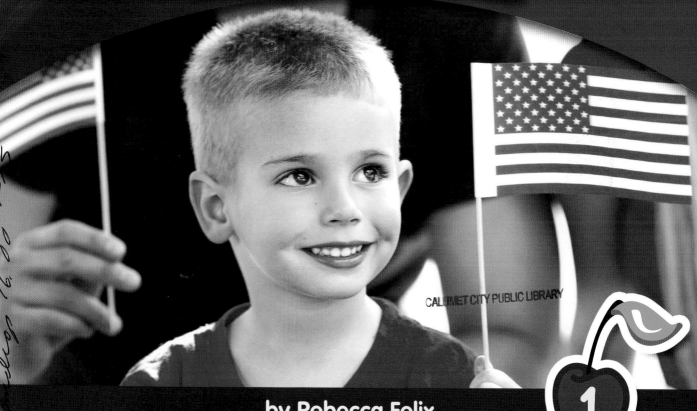

CALUMET CITY PUBLIC LIBRARY

by Rebecca Felix

Cherry Lake Publishing • Ann Arbor, Michigan

1

CHERRY LAKE Publishing

Published in the United States of America
by Cherry Lake Publishing
Ann Arbor, Michigan
www.cherrylakepublishing.com

Consultant: Marla Conn, ReadAbility, Inc.
Editorial direction and book production: Red Line Editorial

Photo Credits: svetikd/iStockphoto, cover, 1; Feng Yu/Shutterstock
Images, 4; Blue Lantern Studio/Corbis, 6; Maxim Anisimov/iStockphoto,
8; B Calkins/Shutterstock Images, 10; Comstock Images/Getty Images/
Thinkstock, 12; jamirae/iStockphoto, 14; Julio Yeste/Shutterstock Images,
16; Sam Ryley/iStock/Thinkstock, 18; Comstock/Stockbyte/Thinkstock, 20

Library of Congress Cataloging-in-Publication Data
Felix, Rebecca, 1984-
  We celebrate Independence Day in summer / by Rebecca Felix.
      pages cm. -- (Let's look at summer)
  Includes index.
  ISBN 978-1-63137-599-6 (hardcover) -- ISBN 978-1-63137-644-3 (pbk.) --
  ISBN 978-1-63137-689-4 (pdf ebook) -- ISBN 978-1-63137-734-1 (hosted
ebook)
  1. Fourth of July--Juvenile literature. 2. Fourth of July celebrations--
Juvenile literature. I. Title.

  E286.A1278 2014
  394.2634--dc23
                                                2014004450

Cherry Lake Publishing would like to acknowledge the work of The
Partnership for 21st Century Skills. Please visit www.p21.org for more
information.

Printed in the United States of America
Corporate Graphics Inc.
July 2014

TABLE OF CONTENTS

JULY

4

Independence Day

4

Holiday

Independence Day is a holiday. It's in summer. It's on July 4.

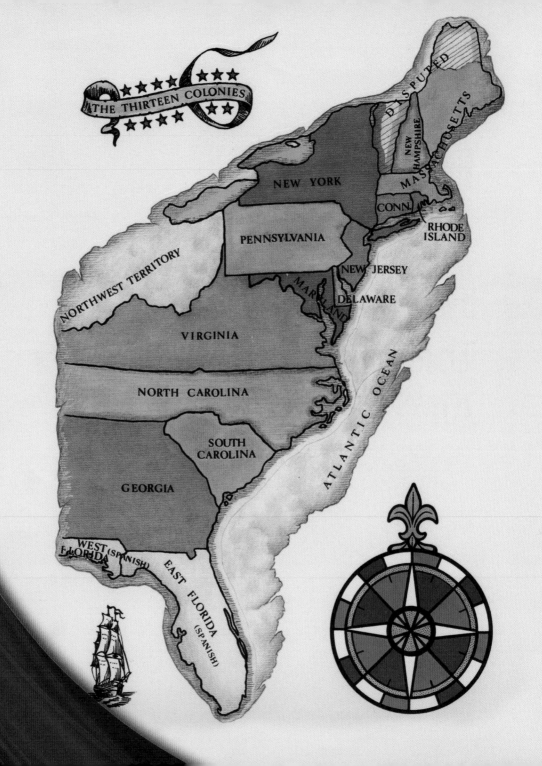

THE THIRTEEN COLONIES

DISPUTED

NEW HAMPSHIRE

MASSACHUSETTS

NEW YORK

CONN.

RHODE ISLAND

PENNSYLVANIA

NEW JERSEY

NORTHWEST TERRITORY

MARYLAND

DELAWARE

VIRGINIA

NORTH CAROLINA

SOUTH CAROLINA

GEORGIA

ATLANTIC OCEAN

WEST (SPANISH) FLORIDA

EAST FLORIDA (SPANISH)

History

July 4, 1776, was special. There were 13 **colonies** in America. Britain ruled them.

The colonies wanted to be free. They came together to form a new nation. The United States was born.

People **celebrate** this day. Many call it the nation's birthday.

What Do You See?

Count the flags.

Food and Fun

People gather on July 4. They have fun. They eat. Some have **picnics**.

13

What Do You See?

The US flag is red, white, and blue.

Some people dress up. They wear the US flag colors.

What Do You See?

Is this car big? Or is it small?

There are many **parades**.

Fireworks

Many people watch **fireworks**!

July 4 is a day of US **pride**.

Find Out More

BOOK

Aloian, Molly. *Independence Day*. New York: Crabtree, 2010.

WEB SITE

Activities and Crafts for July 4th—Enchanted Learning
www.enchantedlearning.com/crafts/july4/
Find fun projects about Independence Day.

Glossary

celebrate (SEL-uh-brate) to enjoy an event or holiday with others

colonies (KAH-luh-nees) areas settled and ruled by another country

fireworks (FYRE-wurks) things that make loud noise and bright light when they explode

parades (puh-RADES) shows moving along streets or areas

picnics (PIK-niks) meals that are eaten outdoors

pride (PRYDE) being pleased or happy with something

Home and School Connection

Use this list of words from the book to help your child become a better reader. Word games and writing activities can help beginning readers reinforce literacy skills.

America	count	holiday	ruled
big	day	Independence	small
birthday	dress	Day	special
blue	eat	July	summer
born	fireworks	nation	together
Britain	flag	new	United States
call	food	parades	wanted
came	free	people	watch
celebrate	fun	picnics	wear
colonies	gather	pride	white
colors	history	red	

What Do You See?

What Do You See? is a feature paired with select photos in this book. It encourages young readers to interact with visual images in order to build the ability to integrate content in various media formats.

You can help your child further evaluate photos in this book with additional activities. Look at the images in the book without the What Do You See? feature. Ask your child to describe one detail in each image, such as a food, activity, or setting.

Index

About the Author

Rebecca Felix is an editor and writer from Minnesota. She celebrates Independence Day by wearing red, white, and blue. Her favorite part of this holiday is watching fireworks!